Musée d'Orsay

PO DE

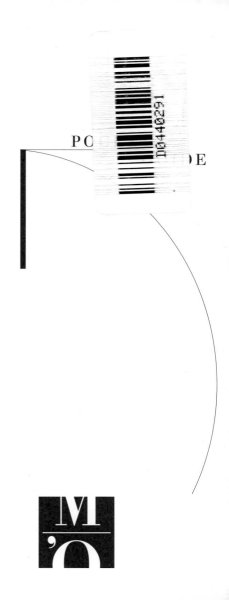

Index

This is a useful small guidebook for your visit.

A well-planned guide already exists for the Musée d'Orsay, providing a comprehensive presentation of all the museum's collections. It calls on the history of art to place the works in their context and gives the necessary background information to help understand the period from 1848 to 1914.

The book which you now hold in your hands is less ambitious but, we hope, just as useful. It is a light work of reference to be kept with you throughout your visit for you to consult while you are in front of the various masterpieces. We have chosen eighty-two works by artists, painters and sculptors, representative of the different trends and periods of that half century in the artistic domain. You can make your own choice among our selection, which follows the normal visitor's circuit in the museum and the numbering of the rooms.

You will find a clear short entry for each of these works, aimed at helping you to improve your understanding of and way of looking at them. The fact that Daumier sculpted parliamentarians from memory after having observed them during sittings in the House, that Bazille painted under the harsh light of Montpellier, or that Camille Claudel represented her personal love and suffering in *L'âge mûr* (Middle Age) is relevant for the understanding of their art: information concerning the artists and their work is included here, but limited to the essential facts. Remarks concerning iconographical or artistic details may also call your attention to some particular aspect of the piece itself where this has seemed necessary.

We hope that this book will help you during your visit and encourage you to prolong it or to come again.

Nicole SAVY
Head of the cultural department

François RUDE

1784 – 1855

Génie de la Patrie

(1836) **The spirit of the motherland**. Some twenty years after the fall of Napoleon I it was decided to complete the Arc de Triomphe begun during the First Empire. Four large high relief sculptures were to decorate the piers of the monument. One of them is François Rude's *Le Départ des volontaires en 1792* (*The departure of the volunteers in 1792*). This exceptionally forceful composition shows a winged spirit, an allegory of the homeland, leading into battle a group of volunteers, prepared to sacrifice themselves to save liberty: in 1792 France had been invaded so the Assembly had declared that the motherland was in danger and called for volunteers, who flocked to Paris from all over the country. «La Marseillaise» was to become their song. The monarchy was overturned, fighting began on the borders, and the victory of Valmy was soon being celebrated.

This head of *La Patrie* (*The Motherland*) has been moulded from the Arc de Triomphe at Place de l'Étoile. An ardent Romantic, Rude used strong contrasts of light and shadow to indicate exaltation. The wide open mouth, the staring eyes, the frowning eyebrows, all reflect the tremendous outburst of patriotism expressed in the French national anthem. This work has given rise to much controversy, directly due to the passions of the revolutionary period: some have described the figure as «a furious termagant», but this head has become a myth under the name «La Marseillaise».

Antoine-Louis BARYE

1796 – 1875

Lion assis

(1847) ***Seated lion.*** Barye is famous for his scenes of fights between wild animals, which number among the most important examples of Romantic sculpture: wild beasts grappling with snakes, jaguars devouring hares, etc.

The imposing size and aspect of this lion is well suited to the representation of an animal which has always symbolised power and majesty. However, Barye did not content himself with extolling the epic character of his subject: he was also a careful observer. At the Jardin des Plantes (the Paris botanical gardens, which include a zoo and the natural history museum) he regularly attended the lectures on comparative anatomy at the natural history museum; like Delacroix, he made drawings of the animals in the zoo and even took measurements from dead wild beasts.

James PRADIER

1790 – 1852

Sapho

(1852) ***Sappho.*** Although this sculpture by Pradier is classical in its treatment of the clothing and face, the attitude of the figure bears witness to a romantic spirit. It represents the poetess Sappho, who lived during the late 7th and early 6th century B.C. on the island of Lesbos, in Greece. She was responsible for a sisterhood of young girls placed under the protection of Aphrodite and the Muses, who studied poetry, music and dance. Her lyrical talents were highly esteemed by the Greeks. In the 20th century she is mainly remembered for her odes in praise of love, beauty and feminine grace. Until the 19th century artists generally represented the moment of her death. According to tradition, she was in love with the shepherd Phaon who scorned her, so she committed suicide by throwing herself into the sea from the top of the Leucadian rock. Pradier alludes to this episode by the waves which cover the base of the statue.

The poetess is represented in meditation, a symbolic figure of that melancholy which, according to romantic tradition, cannot be dissociated from creativity. The lyre beside her helps to give the personage an allegorical dimension: the young woman embodies Poetry itself. Pradier first presented his subject in the form of a small bronze at the 1848 Salon (this was an official exhibition of paintings held annually in Paris). Its success led him to execute a life-size marble statue. The sculptor died just afterwards. The statue was then draped in black crape and thus presented to visitors attending the 1852 Salon.

Jean-Auguste Dominique INGRES

1780 – 1867

La source

(1820-1856) ***The spring.*** In Greek mythology, all nature was inhabited and animated by secondary gods and goddesses. That is why naiads accompany springs. During classical antiquity, they were often depicted leaning on a tilted urn - a tradition which Ingres has called upon in this painting. The young girl personifies the spring, the three trickles of water running from her pitcher adding force to the allegory.

Ingres thus placed this work squarely in the tradition of Neo-Classicism, of which he had been the leading exponent since David's death. He rendered the shape of the female figure in an idealised manner which does away with all natural imperfections. What interested him above all else here are the flowing curves which delicately outline the young girl's figure and echo, as it were, the theme of water.

This painting was compared with the works of the most famous of all Greek sculptors, Phidias. One critic praised the «admirable shape», the «graceful outline» which «attain such a high degree of ideal perfection that none of the candid secrets of this delicate beauty can offend our sense of decency». The figure of the young girl seems to be placed in a recess, and the limited range of colours reinforces the impression of a painted sculpture.

Auguste Préault

1809 – 1879

Ophélie
(model: before 1843 - bronze: 1876) **Ophelia.**

«I am not for the finite, I am for the infinite». This attitude adopted by the sculptor Préault may seem paradoxical if one considers the necessarily finite nature of sculpture, an art which defines itself physically in space with an inherent force, perhaps even more imposing than that of painting since it plays more on the artifices of illusion.

Ophelia is represented after her fatal drowning, drifting with the current. Eyes closed, mouth half open, she has none of the stiffness of death. The relief of the waves mingles with that of the drapery clothing the young girl.

Préault succeeds in arousing the spectator's emotions without calling on exaggeration. A true Romantic, he spurns any reference to classical antiquity. There is no question, as far as he was concerned, of illustrating the feats of famous men, dealing with mythology or using allegories. On the contrary, he has taken his subject from Shakespeare. Most of the Romantic artists were passionate admirers of the author of *Hamlet* and the sad poetic atmosphere which emanates from this sculpture is typical of their interpretation of the playwright's works.

Eugène DELACROIX

1798 – 1863

Chasse aux lions

(1854) ***The lion hunt.*** This *Chasse aux lions* by Eugène Delacroix is a preparatory sketch for a large painting the State commissioned from him in 1854. Rapidly painted, setting down the first rough ideas of his inspiration, it is all the more interesting in that the final painting was partially destroyed by a fire. The theme was inspired by Rubens, as was the composition based on colour and not on draughtsmanship. The vigorous rapid strokes, where the touch of the artist's hand can be sensed, convey the agitation of the scene and the passion of the painter.

The composition is dominated by the rearing horse in the centre. Lions, horses and riders are difficult to make out, especially on the right where the wild beast is braced against the hindquarters of a horse. The dazzling violence of this savage struggle bursts out in the red, green, orange, pink and ochre tones, enhanced by a deep blue. The colours clash in a harmony of which Baudelaire wrote: «Never have more beautiful, more intense colours reached the soul through the eyes». Critics were often opposed to the picture, reproaching Delacroix for the extravagant colours and the incomprehensible nature of the composition. The artist was the last heir of Romanticism, but the importance given here to the coloured masses makes him a precursor. The expressive character of this turmoil heralds the Fauves.

Alexandre CABANEL

1823 – 1889

Naissance de Vénus

(1863) ***The birth of Venus.*** In classical mythology, Venus was born of the sea. The episode has been profusely illustrated from classical antiquity onwards, then again since the Renaissance.

Here, Cabanel depicts the goddess lying on a bed of waves and foam. In a faithful interpretation of mythological tradition, a wreath of Cupids preside over her birth. The painter has chosen a palette of pastel colours, dominated by light pinks and blues. The flesh of Venus has a uniform pearly sheen, suggesting the unreal perfection of porcelain.

The work thus satisfied the criteria of official taste of its time. Presented at the 1863 Salon, it met with such success that Napoleon III purchased it. The same year, Manet was working on a painting which was to give rise to a resounding scandal, *Olympia*. This, on the contrary, depicted a

real woman of her time looking
straight at the spectator. Cabanel's
goddess, voluptuously stretching,
eyes half-closed, may however
now seem more provocative than
Olympia's calm assurance.

Honoré DAUMIER

1808 – 1879

Portraits des célébrités du Juste Milieu

(1831) ***Portraits of the celebrities of the Juste-Milieu.*** Known above all for his caricatures, Daumier was also a painter and sculptor. This portrait gallery represents personalities of his time, especially parliamentarians. To make these «clay snapshots», the artist attended sittings of the House. His extraordinary memory enabled him to register the most characteristic features of his

subjects. He then used modelling to deform, simplify or exaggerate prominent parts of the face such as the nose, forehead or chin. Intent on revealing the moral nature of a person, he ruthlessly showed shortcomings and mannerisms, while retaining the likeness with his model. These caricatural sculptures then served as a basis for his lithographs published in the press.

The title is an ironic reference to a phrase of King Louis-Philippe, as literally «Juste-Milieu» means «the Middle Course»: he considered himself «equally removed from the excesses of popular power and from the abuses of royal power». Being a caricaturist in the 19th century was not without risk. Daumier went to prison for depicting Louis-Philippe as the giant Gargantua in a satirical newspaper.

Jean-François MILLET

1814 – 1875

L'Angélus

(1857-1859) **The Angelus.** Few paintings in the world are as famous as Millet's *Angélus*. Reproduced on all types of objects, it was rapidly known, even in the most remote countryside.

In fact, the subject is very simple and Millet, the best-known of the painters installed at Barbizon, explained it himself: «*L'Angélus* is a picture which I painted while thinking of how, long ago, when working in the fields, my grandmother never failed, on hearing the bell ring, to make us interrupt our task and reverently, with our hats in our hands, say the Angelus for the dead». This is therefore a work filled with nostalgia rather than a mere portrayal of the everyday life Millet could observe on the plain of Chailly, near Barbizon.

From this point of view, *L'Angélus* is a special case, for the Barbizon painters were concerned with depicting reality – of both landscapes and people – a fact which was new for the era. Here, Millet applies himself to rendering the grandeur of the old prayer which recalls the angel's salutation to the Virgin Mary at the Annunciation. In spite of the small size of the picture the man and woman in the foreground have a monumental aspect. They stand out against a sky lit up by the setting sun. The church tower in the distance is tiny, but it is an essential detail, for it is the sound of its bell ringing out across the plain which gives the picture its title.

Camille COROT

1796 – 1875

Une matinée.
La danse des nymphes

(1850) ***Morning. Dance of the
nymphs.*** The poetic visions of
nature painted by Corot were
immensely popular. Here, the
artist seeks a delicate harmony between the figures and the nature
around them. As a setting for this
scene he used a landscape study
made earlier in Italy and transformed it by bathing it in diffused
light. However this dance of the
nymphs is also the souvenir of one
of the artist's daydreams at the
Opera, where he often went and
made numerous sketches of dancers. The airy feeling of the
countryside, where the slight
condensation due to a morning
mist seems about to evaporate, is in
harmony with the delicate figures
celebrating the return of daylight.
On the left a Bacchus-like silhouette raises his cup to the sky.
On the right, a nymph takes another by the hand to lead her to join
their companions' merry dance in
the centre. A soft light illuminates
the whole scene; some of the

foliage is treated with a trans-
parent effect, some in opaque and
moss-like masses.

Corot liked to paint out of doors. He
observed nature carefully, anxious,
he said, «never to lose that first
impression which has affected us».
Although he sometimes continued
to place nymphs in his landscapes,
in the classical tradition, his
studies on light at different times
of the day herald those of the
Barbizon painters. Later, the
Impressionists unanimously
recognised his talent and
influence.

Jean-Baptiste CARPEAUX

1827 – 1875

Ugolin

(1860) ***Ugolino.*** The ambition behind this huge group was the desire to treat a subject inspired by Dante in the manner of Michelangelo.

Count Ugolino, tyrant of Pisa, was imprisoned with his children and condemned to death by starvation; he was reduced to devouring their corpses, which lead to him becoming one of the damned heroes of Dante's *Inferno.* Here, Ugolino laments the ravages hunger has inflicted on his children: «When I recognised my own aspect on their four faces, I bit my hands with grief and my children, believing it was with hunger, suddenly arose saying: Oh, father! It would be less distressing for us if you ate us».

Carpeaux executed this work at the end of his stay at the Villa Medici in Rome. He had presented himself many times for the «Prix de Rome» which entitled him to this stay, for the prize guaranteed a brilliant career and State commissions. Without these many sculptors of modest origin like him could not afford the costly materials they needed to work. The subject of Ugolino was not inspired by classical antiquity, so the piece was not very well received by the Academy. It did however mark the start of a meteoric career for Carpeaux.

Thomas COUTURE

1815 – 1879

Romains de la décadence

(1847) ***Romans of the Decadence.***
«More cruel than war, vice has descended on Rome and avenged the vanquished universe». These lines by the Latin poet Juvenal accompanied the title *Romains de la décadence* in the booklet purchased by visitors to the 1847 Salon, where the public discovered this work, as ambitious by its subject as by its size. On his own confession, Thomas Couture wished «to regenerate French art» by seeking a new way after decades of confrontation between the Neo-Classics, of whom Ingres was the foremost representative, and the Romantics, who claimed Delacroix as their leader.

For this important project, Couture chose a moral subject, inspired by Ancient Rome and which thus satisfied the requirements for what was considered the most noble type of painting. The scene shows an orgy, early in the morning. Drunk, dejected or ill, the guests are reaching the end of their night of debauchery. However, they only occupy the lower section of the painting: above them are seen quite different figures. A series of sculptures evoke the heroes of Republican Rome, seeming silently to reproach the orgy which is coming to an end and the aberrations it induced. On the right, a drunkard even thinks he can fill his cup from the marble amphora held by a statue.

In the company of the two silent spectators contemplating the scene from the lower right-hand corner, Couture incites us to sit in judgement on this debauchery. However, is he denouncing the decadence of Imperial Rome, or that of the July monarchy, which was moribund when the painting was shown? A critic of the time did indeed baptise the work *Les Français de la décadence* (*French of the Decadence*).

Gustave COURBET

1819 – 1877

Un enterrement à Ornans

(1849–1850) ***Burial at Ornans.***
With *Un enterrement à Ornans*
Courbet painted a veritable manifesto for Realism. This artistic
movement, born in France in the
middle of the century as a reaction
to academic art, was generally
associated with social and political
concerns; Courbet, a companion of
the first socialists, was in a way its
torch-bearer.

The realism of this painting lies in the
truthfulness to life of the
representations, of the place –
Courbet's home village – and the
people, who are all identified. The
artist has caught their very
essence, so many of them appear to
be quite ordinary.

Courbet used a format normally
reserved for supposedly noble
subjects to portray simple people in
a scene from everyday life. His
picture created a scandal at the
1850 Salon: «Is it possible to paint
such hideous people?», one critic
asked. Above all, Courbet could
not be forgiven for having dared to

paint humble people in the same way as heroes. And yet, by placing a skull and some bones on the edge of the tomb – a detail which is not consistent with a funeral ceremony – Courbet goes beyond observed reality and seems to invite the spectator to meditate on the question of death. This work, entirely given over to austerity and silence, is also remarkable for its colours: the blacks are all different from one another, enhanced by flashes of white and the strong accents of red robes and blue stockings.

François-Désiré FROMENT-MEURICE

1802 – 1855

Table et garniture de toilette

(1847-1851) ***Dressing table and toilet set.*** This dressing table with its accessories was commissioned in 1845, after a fund was started by a circle of ladies faithful to the so-called «legitimate» branch of the Bourbons, i.e. the family of Charles X, on the occasion of the marriage between the king's grand-daughter, Louise Marie-Thérèse, and the future Duke of Parma.

Before being delivered to the Duchess it was presented at the London Universal Exhibition of 1851, where it was admired for its perfect execution. The result of collaboration between a goldsmith, an architect, an ornamentist and two sculptors, it represents a spectacular combination of materials, rich in references to many civilisations and periods: Islam, the Middle Ages, the Gothic style, Renaissance, Baroque, etc. The fact that bygone techniques which had fallen into disuse were employed also bears witness to the historical nature of this unique set –

for example, the painted enamel, in the manner of the French 16th century, of the small plaques decorating the two caskets.

The result of research carried out in precious metalworking during the 1830s and 1840s, this set today stands revealed as a masterpiece of the eclectic style which was to dominate the decorative arts in France throughout the Second Empire.

Charles-Guillaume DIEHL,
Jean BRANDELY,
Emmanuel FRÉMIET

Médaillier

(1867) ***Medal cabinet.*** This piece of furniture, designed to house a collection of coins or medals, attracted considerable attention at the Paris Universal Exhibition of 1867 and was admired for its imposing aspect and perfect execution.

The cabinet-maker Diehl allowed a large amount of space on his piece of furniture for Frémiet's work. The latter's sculptures, in silvered bronze and copper, go far beyond the ornamental accompaniment generally expected from reliefs decorating furniture. The sources of inspiration for these sculptures belong to French history, and more precisely to the Merovingian period. The central relief represents the triumph of Merovius at Châlons-sur-Marne, where the young Frankish chieftain is said to have crushed his rival, a protégé of Attila. This reference to a glorious past is accompanied by a quest for decorative effects suggestive of antiquity: trophies of arms, although bearing no relationship to authentic mediaeval decorative art, corroborate the remote period of the scene.

For modern spectators this unique masterpiece may seem heavy and pompous; however, it remains the perfect example of an attempt to launch a completely new style in furniture, far removed from the pastiches which were so frequent under the French Second Empire.

Pierre PUVIS DE CHAVANNES

1824 – 1898

Le pauvre pêcheur

(1881) ***The poor fisherman.*** *Le pauvre pêcheur* was the first painting by Puvis de Chavannes to be purchased by the French State. It long exercised a veritable fascination and roused violently hostile reactions, like that of the writer Huysmans who considered it merely «a burlesque of biblical grandeur» and «old fresco painting attacked by moonlight». But it also encountered passionate defenders who considered it «an image of the beauty which lies in everything», or yet again «a poignant image of poverty, despair and misery beyond remedy».

Beauty, despair, misery... his admirers raised the painting to a timeless, mythical state, attained by the sobriety of its pictorial means: an austere composition, the absence of movement and relief, a limited range of colours. The attitudes of the three figures – the fisherman

and his children – seem to be
frozen in a moment of eternity.
Seurat, Maillol and Signac, but also the
Nabis and, later, Picasso, were
influenced by this great work.

Gustave MOREAU

1826 – 1898

Orphée

(1865) ***Orpheus.*** Gustave Moreau drew his inspiration for this scene from the legend of Orpheus. Inconsolable after the death of Eurydice, Orpheus spurned the advances of the Thracian women, who killed him then scattered his dismembered body. His head was carried down to the sea. The painter has interpreted the legend freely, depicting a young girl reverently holding the poet's head.

Absorbed in some mournful daydream, her face is seen in profile, her eyelids lowered as she contemplates this head with its permanently closed eyes. The two faces, mysteriously alike, seem to be linked by some impossible exchange of glances. The young girl's hairstyle and clothing are a mixture of Italy and the Orient; her silhouette stands out against a rocky background reminiscent of Leonardo da Vinci.

Two elements evoke music: the shepherds playing the flute high up on the rock, in the top left corner of the painting, and the tortoises making their way across the ground in the bottom right corner. A tortoise shell, it was said, was used to make the first lyre.

This work, painted in oil on a wood panel, has a strange power of fascination. Proust, who was particularly fond of it, wrote: «We see in this head of Orpheus something which is considering us through those fine blind eyes, imagined colours».

Edgar DEGAS

1834 – 1917

La famille Bellelli

(1858-1867)   *The Bellelli family.*

A masterpiece of Degas' early years, *La famille Bellelli* is one of the largest pictures he ever undertook. The painter's aunt is portrayed here in her home in Florence, accompanied by her children and husband. An evident desire to identify the personages exactly does not suffice to explain the importance given to the setting: this interior is like a stage, giving the work a theatrical tone. The influence of Van Dyck, whose works the artist had admired in Genoa, like that of Holbein, perceptible in the treatment of the female faces, is transcended here: a faithful description of the features of the sitters has ceded the principle role to the drama in which they are actors. The discord between the Bellelli couple is accentuated by the lack of harmony in their attitudes – dignified and motionless for the mother, evasive for the father. Each of the two children seems to reflect one of their parents: the family's dissension is clearly shown by the fact that each person is looking in a different direction.

Édouard MANET

1832 – 1883

Olympia

(1863) ***Olympia***. Painted in 1863,
Olympia is one of Manet's most
famous works. Presented at the
1865 Salon it created a real
scandal. The picture does however
have traditional origins, with two
obvious sources of inspiration:
Titian's *Venus of Urbino* and Goya's
Naked Maja. However the subject,
like its interpretation, greatly
shocked the public.

This is a realistic nude in a
contemporary scene. Manet,
unlike Cabanel for his *Vénus,* did
not resort to any pretext. Olympia
is no mythological creature, but a
prostitute; the scene is not located
in a Turkish harem, but in the Paris
of the artist's time. The naked
woman is a real woman, Victorine
Meurent, a model often used by
Manet. Her body is not idealised.
She was considered ugly and
vulgar. Her nudity is emphasised
by the black ribbon around her
neck and the slipper on her foot.
She looks directly at the spectator
and this quiet assurance was felt to
be intolerably insolent. The black
maid carrying a superb bouquet,

doubtless sent by some client, and the black cat standing at Olympia's feet – a pointed erotic allusion – add to the feeling of unease aroused by the painting.

The manner in which it was painted shocked as much as the subject itself: much was written about the crude and gaudy coulours, the violence and vulgarity of the contrasts! Today, we admire the classic composition of the work, the refined colours, the modern realism of Manet, who stated, with regard to this work: «I did what I saw». At the time Zola was almost the only person to stand up for Manet. He did so enthusiastically, predicting that *Olympia* would find her place in the Louvre. It was to thank him for this encouragement that the artist painted the author's portrait.

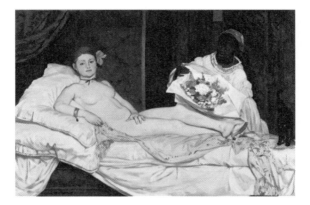

Henri FANTIN-LATOUR

1836 – 1904

Coin de table

(1872) ***The corner of a table.*** Eight people are gathered around a table at the end of a meal. They include, in the left foreground, Paul Verlaine and Arthur Rimbaud, whose presence made the painting famous. The six other guests, contributors to a literary magazine founded in 1872, have now fallen into oblivion. They all had connections with the group of poets known as the Parnassians.

Fantin-Latour's first idea was of a «homage to Baudelaire», a sort of literary pendant to his *Hommage à Delacroix*. Then the figure of Baudelaire disappeared and the work was given the innocuous title of *Coin de table* – a corner of a table with a curious perspective giving the impression of a lack of stability, contrasting with the static poses of the figures. On the right, the end of the table is hidden by a bouquet. Was this intended to take the place of some guest who refused to appear in the supposedly discreditable company of Verlaine and Rimbaud?

Nowadays this painting, quite apart

from its aesthetic value, represents for us a testimony regarding the literary history of the 19th century. Its format is that of a historical painting rather than of a simple everyday scene. And that is precisely what some critics did not accept in 1872: «Who can have advised Mr Fantin-Latour to give his *Coin de table* such epic and monumental proportions? ... There is a contradiction between the ambitious size of the canvas and its subject which in the long term becomes exasperating», they wrote.

Eugène BOUDIN

1824 – 1898

La plage de Trouville

(1865) *The beach at Trouville.*

Born at Honfleur, a small port in Normandy, Eugène Boudin painted some three hundred scenes of beaches. As one contemporary critic wrote: «Mr Boudin has invented a type of seascape which is his alone». In 1862 he moved to Trouville, a fishing village which had recently become a fashionable seaside resort. In this picture a stylish and elegant crowd is shown as if in a frieze on a narrow strip of sand, whereas a cloudy sky occupies the greater part of the painting. The ladies' dresses are enhanced with touches of bright colours and contrast with the long silhouettes of the men, clothed in black. The painter has chosen a fairly low viewpoint, so the surroundings are not visible, except for a scrap of sea in the centre. The wind does however make its presence felt. The people and the small black dog in the foreground are straining against it.

The impression of a scene painted from life, of the movement of air and light, make Boudin a precursor of Impressionism. It was moreover he who introduced Monet to working out of doors. Boudin's skies were greatly admired by Baudelaire, who spoke of «liquid and aerial magic» when referring to them, and Corot, who called Boudin «the king of skies».

Claude MONET

1840 – 1926

La pie

(1868-1869) ***The magpie.***

During the winter of 1868-1869, Monet stayed at Etretat, from where he wrote to his friend Bazille: «I travel around the countryside which is so beautiful here, which I find perhaps even more agreeable in the winter than in the summer, and naturally I am working (...) I think that this year I will do some serious things». This was when he painted *La pie*, a serious work indeed by both its relatively large size and the smooth aspect of its surface, in spite of the free manner of painting used.

Monet had already painted other landscapes of the snow-covered countryside – it was in fact a fashionable subject during the 1860s. However, painters generally dwelt on the impression of lethargy and desolation it gave the landscape. Monet turned it into something vibrant, alive with light, a landscape which surprises by the refinement and diversity of its range of whites. White, but above all yellow, blue, mauve, the snow is set off by the black touch added by the magpie, the point of equilibrium of the picture.

Frédéric BAZILLE

1841 – 1870

Réunion de famille

(1867) *A family reunion.* Frédéric Bazille was twenty-six when he decided to paint this large picture in his family home at Méric, near Montpellier. He gathered all the members of his family, including himself on the far left, under the chestnut tree on the terrace. The many intent gazes and a certain stiffness in the poses of its members confers a fixed and solemn expression on this group, contrasting with the originality of the composition.

The picture shows how sensitive Bazille was to the harsh southern light which separates the planes distinctly and accentuates contrasts and the solidity of forms. The light passing through the foliage changes the colours of the clothes and the ground while clearly revealing the group's faces.

The painting was accepted for the 1868 Salon. Two years later the young artist – close to the future Impressionists – was killed during the Franco-Prussian war.

Claude MONET

1840 – 1926

Femmes au jardin

(1867) ***Women in a garden.*** In 1866, Monet rented a house in Ville-d'Avray and began *Femmes au jardin*, which he completed a year later. Instead of working in his studio from preparatory sketches he painted directly out of doors. He had a trench dug in the garden where he could lower the canvas by means of a pulley in order to work on the upper section while retaining the same viewpoint. When visiting him Courbet once expressed his surprise at finding him idle. Monet replied that he was waiting for the sun, thus revealing his principal concern, which was to render the exact effect of light, trusting in what he could see without being influenced by what he knew.

In this open-air scene the figures stand out clearly against a background of greenery. His companion, Camille, posed for the four female silhouettes, whose faces are not greatly individualised. Large patches of sunlight and shadow are placed side by side, with no transition between them. The light-coloured stylised dresses have the stiffness of the fashion plates from which they are copied. The slight twirling movement of the young red-haired woman on the right gives an impression of depth. The very free manner of painting, the bold off-centre framing of the scene, the contrasts of light, were all violently criticised and the work was refused by the jury for the 1867 Salon.

25

Jean-Baptiste Carpeaux

1827 – 1875

Le prince impérial et son chien Néro

(1865) **The Prince Imperial and his dog Nero**. This marble sculpture portrays the son of Napoleon III and the Empress Eugénie, accompanied by his dog.

Carpeaux knew his model well, as he had become the young prince's drawing master. The prince posed in the Orangery at the Tuileries palace, replaced for some of the time by a child of the same age for Carpeaux to make drawings from the nude and study the skeleton and muscles.

Carpeaux has not shown the prince in an official pose but almost familiarly, in his everyday clothes. The child has his arm affectionately round the dog's neck.

The artist hoped this sculpture would greatly help his future. The portrait pleased the monarchs. «The Empress came to see me yesterday with a large suite. My success is guaranteed and the bravos filled me with joy.» The Emperor commissioned the marble version, which was placed in the

Tuileries palace. In 1870 the Imperial family took it with them into exile in England. A scaled-down version of the work, produced by the Sèvres Manufacture in 1869, continued to be marketed after 1870 under the title *L'enfant au chien* (*Child with a dog*).

26

Jean-Baptiste CARPEAUX

1827 – 1875

La Danse

(1863-1869) ***The Dance.*** In 1863
Charles Garnier, the architect of
the new Paris opera house, commissioned four large groups of
sculpture from different artists to
decorate the façade of the building.
Carpeaux was responsible for illustrating the theme of dance. He
spent three full years making
numerous sketches and models
before conceiving this swirling
farandole of women encircling the
personification of Dance. On the
ground a Cupid is rattling a bauble,
or jester's emblem. On the right,
behind the dancers, a satyr's grin-
ning face can be glimpsed. The
main preoccupation of Carpeaux
was to render the impression of
movement. He did so by means of
a dual dynamic force, simultaneously vertical and circular.
The leaping personification of
Dance dominates the group; he is
shaking a tambourine to draw the
maenads into the whirl. His andro-
gynous silhouette and face contrast
with the full figures of the dancers.
They are shown in various attitudes, off balance, the tips of their

toes barely touching the ground. This instability is reinforced by the oblique lines of the legs.

Whereas Garnier greatly admired this composition, the public, for its part, was shocked, in particular by the realism of the bodies. A bottle of ink was thrown at the group and the scandal was such that its removal was demanded. However the war of 1870, then the death of Carpeaux, put an end to the controversy. In 1964 the stone was threatened by the effects of pollution, so a copy made by Paul Belmondo was installed on the Opéra and the original brought into the museum.

Charles GARNIER

1825 – 1898

Opéra de Paris

(1860-1875) *Paris opera house.*

Charles Garnier, winner of the competition announced in 1860 for the construction of an opera house in Paris, designed a building which is all curves and monumental exuberance. He wanted the distribution of the internal volumes to be perceptible from outside.

On the right, the entrance hall occupies the first section of the building. It is crowned by the large foyer. Decorated with mirrors and painted ceilings, this communicates with the double colonnaded loggia which forms the external façade. The second section of the building is entirely occupied by the great staircase; on each floor there are balconies over which members of the audience can lean.

In the centre of the building, under the copper dome, is the red and gold Italian-style auditorium with its original ceiling, now concealed by the one painted by Chagall. Further to the left, in the tallest part of the building, is the slightly sloping stage. Complex machinery enables the scenery to be changed. Beyond this the richly decorated dance foyer is reserved for the performers. Finally, at the back, are the administrative offices.

On either side of the main part of the building are two small domed pavilions. One is the entrance for season-ticket holders; the other, preceded by a gentle double slope permitting the access of a horse-drawn carriage, leads to Napoleon III's box. In fact, its originally designated occupier was never to take possession of it: the new opera house was only inaugurated in 1875, five years after the fall of the Second Empire.

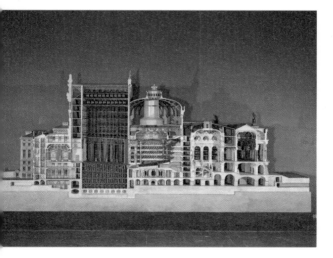

Koloman MOSER

1868 – 1918

Armoire à musique

(c. 1904) **Music cabinet**. At the beginning of the century this music cabinet furnished the Viennese drawing room of the Wittgenstein family, which many great composers - Brahms, Richard Strauss and Mahler, among others - had frequented, or continued to visit.

Koloman Moser, who was also a painter, illustrator and interior decorator, drew his inspiration for this piece from the clear-cut designs of furniture by the Scottish architect Mackintosh, very subtly interpreted. Ceruse white was applied to the oak before it was lacquered to bring out the veins of the wood; the presence of plaques of silver metal on the doors accentuates the precious nature of the cabinet, which is otherwise restrained, even austere. A projecting gilded edging, like the ripple of a musical vibration, does however alleviate its bulky aspect. This piece of furniture was made by the *Wiener Werkstätte,* or Viennese Workshops, an association of artists and designers whose aim was to encourage the production of quality craftwork in order to combat the mediocrity of industrially produced objects. These designs remained very expensive and their strict aesthetic style mainly concerned a world of enlightened and well-off connoisseurs.

Édouard MANET

1832 – 1883

Le déjeuner sur l'herbe

(1863) At the time Manet was painting *Le déjeuner sur l'herbe* (literally, «Lunch on the grass», or «The picnic»), artistic life was dominated by an annual event: the Salon. This was an official exhibition where artists were invited to present their most recent work. Its repercussions were far-reaching, since it attracted up to five hundred thousand visitors, or the equivalent of over a quarter of the population of Paris; the prizes distributed there were decisive for artists' careers. It was therefore essential to be accepted to exhibit there. However, selection was drastic: in 1863 the admissions jury refused over half the works presented, including this painting by Manet, at the time called *Le bain* (*Bathing*). The protests were such that Napoleon III decided that the works which had been rejected should also be exhibited. The «Salon des réfusés» became the comic attraction of Paris. The public were convulsed with laughter, in particular in front of this painting by Manet, who was accused of flaunting depraved tastes: showing a naked modern woman, without the slightest mythological pretext and in the company of clothed men, seemed to be the height of indecency.

Manet became famous overnight, but he was deeply wounded by these reactions. There was however a certain degree of provocation in this picture, where the landscape is treated in a rapid, almost off-hand, manner, in contrast with the still life in the foreground and, especially, with the pale-skinned, dark-eyed naked woman, surrounded by men clothed in black. To be sure, Manet here took up a theme already exploited by Raphael and Titian but, arriving in his own fashion at Courbet's realism, he executed a work which is more coarse than sensual, with a very novel vision of painting.

Gustave CAILLEBOTTE

1848 – 1894

Raboteurs de parquet

(1875) **The planers.** *Raboteurs de parquet* remains Caillebotte's most famous painting. It is easy to see how carefully and with what attention to fact the artist observed the planers' work. They first damped the floor, then passed the plane over the joins of the floorboards before smoothing the wood with a scraper in such a way as to obtain a perfectly even and light-coloured surface. Sometimes they had to hammer in a few pegs or sharpen their tools. Then, when it was time for a break, a glass of wine put fresh heart into their work. The setting is a room in a fine apartment of a Paris building dating from Haussmann's urbanisation period.

This interest in the life of common people, in this case small trades or craftsmen, was exactly contemporary with that of Zola when he described, for example, the work of the ironers in *L'Assommoir* (*The Dram Shop*).

Caillebotte was a friend of the Impressionists and collected their works, although his way of painting was quite different. This picture was in fact included in the second Impressionist exhibition in 1876, when the critics considered the subject unusual and vulgar.

What still surprises us nowadays, apart from the very fine study of light and reflections, is the viewpoint chosen by Caillebotte: a high angle, which gives the spectator the impression of standing in front of the planers. The space is strictly structured and demarcated: the rectilinear lay-out of the boards makes the floor omnipresent and defines a strong perspective.

Edgar DEGAS

1834 – 1917

*Dans un café
ou L'absinthe*

(c. 1875-1876) ***In a café***, or
Absinth. This scene of modern life
combines a naturalistic theme with
a double portrait for which Degas
had two close friends sit. The
atmosphere of gloom and listless-
ness given off by this painting calls
to mind Émile Zola's *L'Assommoir*
(*The Dram Shop*). Seated side by
side, the couple are silent and seem
to ignore each other: she has a
fixed disillusioned stare, he averts
his eyes as if to avoid her. Their
despondency can be seen on their
faces, their interior solitude is
obvious. It was the novelty of the
subject, drawn from contemporary
life and treated without compla-
cency, which created a scandal,
even more than the technique,
deemed «off-hand».

The mastery of Degas is however
obvious in the composition: the off-
centre framing calls to mind
photography, in which the painter
was interested. The tables and the
newspapers wrapped around their
rods, underlined by the painter's

signature, form a play on oblique lines reminiscent of the type of perspective inspired by Japanese art, creating an empty space in the foreground. The wan light coming from the right is reflected by the mirror where two blackish shadows can be seen. Among the dull colours of the scene the weak green gleam of the glass of absinth shines out.

32

Edgar DEGAS

1834 – 1917

La classe de danse

(c. 1873-1876) ***The ballet class.***

From the 1870s onwards dancers gave Degas inspiration for countless drawings, paintings and pastels. He was more interested in attitudes during classes and rehearsals than by appearances on the stage. His concern with breaking down movements is especially evident in his small sculptures. *La classe de danse*, a painting begun in 1873, required more than two years' work.

The picture is swarming with details which suggest the class is ending, in particular the exhaustion and distracted mood of the resting dancers. Practically none are paying any attention to their old master, and even less so the two ballerinas who dominate the others at each end of the room – one, in the background, is adjusting the ribbon around her neck, whereas the other, seated on the piano in the foreground, is scratching her back.

The painter has adopted a slightly raised viewpoint. Because of this the perspective, accentuated by the receding lines of the floor, rises sharply. The floor occupies more than a quarter of the composition, creating an empty space in the centre of which is the dancing master. Around him the white gauze tutus studded with their brightly coloured bows enliven a space which is given great depth by the play on perspective.

33

Edgar Degas

1834 – 1917

*Petite danseuse
de quatorze ans*
(1879-1881) ***The little dancer
aged fourteen.*** This bronze sculpture was cast after the artist's death.
The wax original, now in the USA,
is the most important sculpture by
Degas. It was the only one exhibited during his lifetime, at the sixth
Impressionist exhibition in 1881.
Degas had worked on it for three
years.

He had begun making sculptures by the
1860s. They helped him to catch
forms in three dimensions when
composing his paintings. However,
this little dancer is not a study but a
finished work, bearer of the artist's
ambitions. Scrupulously realistic,
even more so in the wax original
because the polychromy renders
the colour of her flesh, this dancer
has been dressed in a tulle tutu
with a pink satin ribbon in her hair.
The original also had doll's hair, a
blouse and real ballet shoes.

This sculpture produced an
extraordinary effect. According to
one critic, no prior warning could

have prepared the spectator for its realism. With regard to this work, Huysmans wrote: «Mr Degas has overturned the traditions of sculpture, as he has, for a long time, upset the conventions of painting».

It was however the physical appearance of the dancer, a young model aged fourteen, which above all set the critics off and created a scandal. «Her coarse insolence» and «her forehead, like her lips,

marked with a profoundly vicious character» were remarked upon. With this work, Degas went beyond realism to become, in a way, the ethnologist of the Parisian lower classes.

34

Alfred SISLEY

1839 – 1899

*L'inondation
à Port-Marly*

(1876) ***Floods at Port-Marly.***
Alfred Sisley painted this landscape at Port-Marly in 1876 when the Seine was in flood. In spite of the atmosphere of desolation due to the subject itself, the picture radiates a certain serenity. The composition is closed on the left by the bar, «at the sign of St Nicholas», and open on the right. The building is the only stable element. Its permanence, accentuated by its frontal representation, contrasts with the prevailing impression of flowing movement.

The colours contribute to the harmony and refinement: the blue and ochre of the house, seen again in its reflection, but also in the countless touches making up the sky and the water. The sky was Sisley's principal concern, and he always began his landscapes there.

This flood on the Seine was a source of inspiration for several paintings, including *La barque pendant l'inondation (The boat during the flood)*, painted from a slightly different viewpoint at a more sunny moment.

35

Camille Pissarro

1830 – 1903

Les toits rouges, coin de village, effet d'hiver

(1877) *The red roofs, a corner of a village, winter effect.* Using small brushstrokes, Pissarro has covered his canvas with a thick layer of paint, and obtained a beautifully dense effect. This technique was new for him; he had until then worked rather with light paint, a little in the manner of Corot. Since his move to Pontoise in 1872 - he stayed there more than ten years - and his encounter with Paul Cézanne, he was more inclined to use a heavy grainy paste which he did not smooth out on his support.

This corner of a village is a pretext for a chromatic study: it is the red roofs which interest the painter and which are the true subject of the picture, if its title, which is probably the original one, can be trusted. This red is set off by a series of harmoniously distributed green touches: it is the end of the winter, the fields are beginning to show a little colour. The trees, still

leafless, generate a blurred effect which makes the opaque mass of the houses stand out in contrast.
This work belonged to the painter Gustave Caillebotte, a companion and patron of the Impressionists. When he died, he bequeathed his collection to the French State. This bequest, which included many pictures which are now famous but were at the time controversial, gave rise to much argument. The State finally made a choice and *Les toits rouges* was among the works retained.

36

Claude MONET

1840 – 1926

Régates à Argenteuil

(c. 1872) *Regatta at Argenteuil.*
The bright luminosity of this work
is due to the use of pure colours,
which seem to come «straight out
of the tube». Until then, painters
made their own colours up from
powders and carried them around
in pigs' bladders. The invention of
paint in tubes, towards the middle
of the 19th century, made working
out of doors, or «painting from
nature», much easier.

In order to paint these sails at
Argenteuil, Claude Monet may
have set his easel up in the boat-
studio which he had built in order
to work on the water. The
reflection of the landscape troubled
by the lapping of the water
interested him as much, if not
more, than the view itself. The
broad brushstrokes used to paint
the reflection transcribe the
fragmentation due to the
movement of the water.

«I am running after a block of colour»,
Monet wrote. «I want to reproduce

something elusive. It is dreadful, this light which disappears, taking colour with it.»

The fashion for yachting and the construction of two railway lines contributed to the development of Argenteuil, a small suburban town situated on the banks of the Seine. Early in the 1870s Manet, Monet, Renoir, Sisley and Caillebotte lived there or met each other there to work together. The Argenteuil period was fundamental in the history of Impressionism.

37

Claude MONET

1840 – 1926

La gare Saint-Lazare

(1877) ***St Lazare railway station.***
This view of St Lazare railway station in Paris by Claude Monet belongs to a series of twelve paintings, seven of which were presented at the third Impressionist exhibition in 1877. This eminently modern subject had already been tackled by Manet and Caillebotte, but they only remained in the vicinity of the station. Monet requested and obtained permission from the manager of the French western region railway company to set his easel up inside this station with which he, like all his painter friends, was already familiar as a passenger.

Concerning these works, Zola wrote: «This year Monet exhibited some superb station interiors. You can hear the rumble of the trains disappearing into them, see the clouds of smoke billowing around. That is where painting lies today. Our artists must discover the poetry of stations as their forefathers did that of forests and rivers».

Under the glass roof of the station and

beyond it, towards the Europe bridge which can be perceived in the background, Monet studied variations of light. The yellows and oranges of the buildings and the tracks set off the whole range of blues and violets which predominate in the wreaths of smoke. The painted surface is rough. The small irregular brushstrokes follow the movements of the smoke and the vibrations of the light.

The shapes disintegrate in the light and, at the same time, the artist's preoccupation with a meticulous composition is evident in this painting. A study in a sketchbook does moreover bear witness to this attention to detail.

38

Pierre-Auguste RENOIR

1841 – 1919

Bal du Moulin de la Galette, Montmartre

(1876) ***Dancing at Moulin de la Galette, Montmartre.*** At the third exhibition of the Impressionist group in 1877 Renoir's *Bal du Moulin de la Galette* attracted much attention. Modern life, the open air, a lively crowd, carefree amusements, the play on light, the rich colours, the versatile and rapid brushstrokes, all the ingredients of the new style were combined here and reached fulfilment.

The «guingettes», popular open-air cafés with music and dancing, were a favourite subject for painters wishing to depict numerous moving figures with bright patches of sunlight filtering through leaves. Renoir strived to express the jaunty attitudes and cheerful atmosphere. «To my way of thinking», he said, «a picture should be something which is pleasant, happy and pretty, yes: pretty. There are enough disagreeable things in life for us not to make any more of them.»

This picture does not give the

impression of having been composed or arranged. The figures form shifting groups, cut off by the edges of the canvas; the touch is swift and elongated, the brushstrokes blend gently into one another. It all gives the feeling of an impromptu work based on a quick glimpse. However, this spontaneity is merely apparent: Renoir in fact devoted the whole of the summer of 1876 to this painting.

Far from sharing in the pleasure this picture arouses in today's public, the critics of the time considered it excessively daring. One of them wrote: «It looks like freshly painted canvas over which pistachio, vanilla and red-currant flavoured creams have been spread».

39

Claude MONET

1840 – 1926

Les *Cathédrales de Rouen*

(1892-1894) The ***Rouen Cathedral*** series. With five versions of *La cathédrale de Rouen*, the Musée d'Orsay has a good example of the series which Claude Monet inaugurated with his *Meules* (*Haystacks*) in 1890, based on the representation of a single subject transformed by the weather, the light, the time of day or the season. The *Cathedral* series numbers thirty works. In order to paint them, Monet successively occupied several apartments overlooking the cathedral, turning them into studios. He had several canvases in progress and worked on them in turn, depending on the time of day and the light: the sun rises behind Tour Saint Romain on the left and silhouettes the building; then it inundates the façade, lighting it up gradually until the beginning of the afternoon when the whole building seems to shimmer. Finally the shadows rise from the square,

while the setting sun shines on the upper sections. These variations in the light are added to changes in the viewpoint, frontal or oblique, on the same level or looking down. The same façade seen from a different angle seems to move, disintegrate, lean forwards or backwards. It is not the building which interested Monet, but the play of light on the stone.

During his two stays in Rouen Monet devoted all his time to his work: «Each day I add and surprise something which I hadn't yet been able to see»; but he was often beset by doubts: «Alas, I can only repeat this: the more I advance, the more I find it difficult to render what I feel».

For a long time after his return to Giverny he refused to show these paintings, working on them again until the end of 1894 before signing and dating them. In 1895 all thirty were shown at Durand-Ruel's gallery before being dispersed.

40

Auguste RENOIR

1841 – 1919

Jeunes filles au piano

(1892) ***Young girls at the piano.*** In 1891 Renoir was fifty when the State, at the instigation of the poet Stéphane Mallarmé, decided to buy an important recent painting from him. He set to work. A close friend later recounted: «I remember the endless pains he took to execute the official commission for a painting which a well-intentioned friend had exerted himself to obtain for him. It was *Jeunes filles au piano*. Renoir began this painting five or six times, almost identically each time. The very idea of a commission was enough to paralyse him and make him lose all confidence in himself». There are indeed six versions of these *Jeunes filles au piano*; this one is the most finished and, as Renoir himself admitted, is perhaps too polished.

Neither the subject – a sweet and charming picture of a middle class interior – nor the discreet and harmonious composition were now likely to scare off a public shocked by early Impressionism. In addition, the artist used warm soft colours which give a golden tone to the whole, banishing the blue modelling for the shadows which had been the subject of such violent criticism twenty years earlier.

41

Paul CÉZANNE

1839 – 1906

La maison du pendu

(1873) ***The house of the hanged man.*** *La maison du pendu* was one of Cézanne's contributions to the first Impressionist exhibition organised in 1874 as a result of a split with the official Salon system. It depicts a house in the village of Auvers-sur-Oise where Cézanne had come to live two years earlier on the advice of his friend Pissarro. The two painters often worked together in the Oise valley, painting the same subjects. Under Pissarro's influence Cézanne's style developed in a decisive manner. He did not completely abandon the violent and sensual subjects of his early work, but landscapes came to play an important role, bringing with them the choice of a lighter palette and more strictly balanced compositions.

The bold lay-out of *La maison du pendu* calls to mind Courbet and his sturdy landscapes lacking a skyline, just as much as Pissarro's example. The picture has the same rustic tang and solid foundations as the masonry which it depicts. These houses, situated on a bend along a sloping path, seem to be deserted, which makes them appear to be all the more rooted in the undulating ground of the landscape. They occupy almost the whole of the space and the high horizon reinforces their strong presence.

For Cézanne juxtaposing colours was a means of exalting shapes as solid forms and not one of breaking them down into the vibrations of light as the Argenteuil group of painters did. It is in that respect that the distance is greatest between Cézanne and Impressionism. In fact, he was really only linked to Impressionism for the period covering the group's first three exhibitions, until 1877.

42

Paul CÉZANNE

1839 – 1906

Pommes et oranges

(c. 1895-1900) ***Apples and oranges.*** This still life intrigues by the number of elements composing it: the tablecloth with its broken and crushed folds out of which the fruit dish emerges, the heavy drapery in the background, the flower-patterned jug which creates a perfect transition between the drapery and the arrangement of the fruit on the pearly expanse of the tablecloth.

The eye happily follows the complex lines of this dynamic composition. On the spot near the plate where the picture's diagonals cross is an apple, apparently about to fall. It seems to be the epicentre of a sense of imbalance which it imparts to the whole work. Everything seems to be tilting forwards, the notion of depth becomes indistinct, no horizontal lines are perceptible.

This still life, dating from a fairly late period of Cézanne's work, is more complex than the earlier ones: the table and wall no longer construct space, indeed they have disappeared, making way for a new perspective, looking down on the objects and showing them from several viewpoints simultaneously. That is how Cézanne opened the way for Cubism.

43

Paul Cézanne

1839 – 1906

La femme à la cafetière

(c. 1890-1895) **Woman with a coffee-pot.** *La femme à la cafetière* is one of Cézanne's most curious portraits. The model, seen in full face, is seated next to a table on which are placed a coffee-pot and a cup. Her thick features, intent gaze and awkwardly idle hands point to a woman of the lower classes.

The identity of the sitter is not known, and indeed the painter makes no effort to bestow any personality on her, nor to render her feelings or emotions. He gives preference to the geometric relationships between the woman and the objects: the vertical line of the central pleat of her dress is echoed in that bisecting the handle of the teaspoon, and, similarly, both the dress and the coffee-pot are divided by a horizontal line.

These points of comparison accentuate the person's hieratic, or stately, aspect, the impression of mystery and interior strength emanating from her. This portrait is treated in the manner of a still life, and the figure thus acquires a spectacularly monumental character. And yet, the upright attitude of the person and the severity of the setting are gainsaid by the deliberate lack of regularity of the linear network in the background. As in the still lifes of his late period, Cézanne does not hesitate to introduce even into his most structured portraits this slight instability to express his experience of reality, constantly in movement.

44

Henri de TOULOUSE-LAUTREC

1864 – 1901

Panneaux pour la baraque de la Goulue à la foire du Trône à Paris

(1895) ***Panels for La Goulue's booth at the Paris «Foire du Trône».*** In 1895 Henri de Toulouse-Lautrec painted for La Goulue, a famous quadrille dancer he had met at the Moulin-Rouge in Montmartre, these two scenes intended to decorate the entrance of the booth she had hired at the Foire du Trône (an annual fair in Paris). It is miraculous that these two paintings escaped destruction, not only because they were originally presented in the open air but also because they were later cut up into several pieces. The resulting puzzle was only put together again in 1930 and the works restored, but the marks are still visible today.

One of the panels evokes La Goulue's past at the Moulin-Rouge: a small round coloured silhouette, she is dancing with Valentin le Désossé («the boneless»), a strange, dark and dislocated puppet. Around them the regular attendants form a circle; in the background the extravagant plumed hat of Jane Avril, herself a famous dancer, can be recognised.

The other panel shows «the Moorish dance», the new show which La Goulue presented in her booth at the Foire du Trône. The musicians around her are wearing turbans and costumes inspired by some imagined Orient. Among the spectators in the foreground, painted in a spirited caricatural manner, the broad back of the author Oscar Wilde, Jane Avril's hat and the painter himself, seen from behind and tiny under his bowler hat, stand out.

45

Vincent Van Gogh

1853 – 1890

La chambre de Van Gogh à Arles

(1889) ***Van Gogh's bedroom in Arles.*** «I have done (...) a painting (...) of my bedroom. Well, it amused me greatly to do this empty interior. In flat tints, but boldly painted, with a full brush, the walls light lilac, the floor a patchy and faded red, the chairs and bed chrome yellow, the pillows and sheet very pale lime, the blanket blood-red, the dressing table more orange, the washbasin blue, the window green. I wanted to express absolute rest by all these very varied tones where the only white is the little note introduced by the black-framed mirror.»

Van Gogh wrote this letter to his friend Gauguin whom he invited to join him. Vincent had come to live in Arles a few months earlier. There, he had discovered the light of the Midi, or south of France. After painting very dark works in his Dutch youth, his palette had grown lighter during his stay in Paris, under the influence of the Impressionists. Now, in Provence, he used most vivid colours.

«I wanted to express absolute rest.»

Van Gogh's sentence is tinged with a shade of regret. It is indeed rather a vision of anguished solitude which seems to emanate from the sloping floor and tilting walls.

Gauguin's visit ended dramatically: Vincent cut his own ear off in a fit of madness and asked to be interned in the hospital in St Rémy. Since his painting had been damaged, he made two copies, at a time when this room had become just a memory for him. This is the second of them.

46

Vincent Van Gogh

1853 – 1890

Portrait de l'artiste

(1889) *Portrait of the artist.*

«Portraits painted by Rembrandt go beyond nature, they are more like a revelation», Van Gogh wrote. Like Rembrandt, he often used himself as a model: for his ten years of creative activity, there are around forty selfportraits, of which this is one of the last.

The pale bony face is shown in three-quarters profile, turned to the left. This makes the hard, angular features stand out, with the prominent cheekbones, hollow cheeks and eyes set deeply into their sockets. The shades of blue, in a very light key, spread over the whole surface of the picture, blurring the distinction between the figure and the background; the red hair and beard act as counterpoint. The sitter's immobility contrasts with the swirls of the long brushstrokes; the dynamic rhythm of their flame-like forms evokes a world of hallucinations.

The relentlessly intent gaze is striking. Its steadiness expresses deep anxiety, accentuated by the sickly green around the eyes, but there is also an impression of unparalleled will and strength.

47

Vincent VAN GOGH

1853 – 1890

L'église d'Auvers-sur-Oise, vue du chevet

(1890) ***The church at Auvers-sur-Oise, view of the apse.*** After his internment in the Saint-Rémy-de-Provence asylum, Van Gogh returned to the Paris region. He moved to Auvers-sur-Oise, to live with Dr Gachet, a specialist in mental illnesses who was also an art collector and friend of the Impressionists. Van Gogh brought back with him from Provence the memory of Mediterranean light. However, while the sun seems to inundate the vicinity of the church, casting a distinct shadow on the paths in the foreground, the very dark sky creates the effect of a night scene. «I have a large picture of the village church, with an effect where the building seems to have a purplish hue against a plain dark blue sky of pure cobalt; the stained-glass windows stand out like ultramarine blue spots, the roof is violet and partly orange. In the foreground, a little greenery with flowers and some pink sunlit sand.» Van Gogh chose to depict not the façade of the church but its apse. The building is thus seen from the back, like the peasant woman walking away. The brushstrokes are thick and firm, short and jagged; colour and outline become indissociable.

The swirling shapes with the expressive and magnificent colour transform this peaceful church, painted just a month before the artist's suicide, into a dramatic topic.

48

Henri ROUSSEAU

called Le Douanier

1844 – 1910

La charmeuse de serpents

(1907) **The snake-charmer.** The enigmatic silhouette of a woman stands out against the light in a peaceful and luxuriant landscape. This dark, seemingly faceless, Venus is luring birds to herself and taming the wild beasts of the forest.

The fanciful exoticism of this jungle owes nothing to any travels in far-off lands. The artist's nickname, «Le Douanier», or customs officer, is due to the job he held for several years at the Paris customs barrier. Although he claimed the contrary, he seems never to have left France. In fact, the sources of inspiration for his many jungles were often found in the capital itself, in the Jardin des Plantes (botanical gardens) or the natural history museum.

Having become famous through having fun poked at him each year in the press reviews of the Salon des Indépendants, this self-taught artist attracted the attention of many painters and poets, including

Vallotton, Jarry and, later, Picasso, Apollinaire and Robert Delaunay, who persuaded his mother to buy *La charmeuse de serpents*. The same features of Le Douanier's art which shocked some attracted his young admirers: a totally fresh vision which metamorphosed the themes to which it was applied, vivid pure colours, a firm style of drawing and bold compositions. As a matter of fact, it is not certain that the artist, eager for fame and recognition, deliberately turned his back on the conventions of academic painting. His work is designated as «naive» art.

49

Paul GAUGUIN

1848 – 1903

La belle Angèle

(1889) *Beautiful Angèle.* In Pont-Aven, a small town in Brittany, where he lived with a group of painters who shared in his studies, Gauguin began the portrait of Angèle Satre, the mayor's wife. The painter did not embark on a faithful interpretation of the features of the person known throughout the region as «la belle Angèle», or «beautiful Angèle». Breaking with the aesthetic principles of the Impressionists, Gauguin divided his canvas into distinct sections. Angèle's portrait is inscribed within a circle, beside which her name is written in full, as if she were a saint in an icon.

Dressed in the traditional Breton costume which clearly establishes her origins, Angèle seems just as much to be made of stone as the Polynesian statue shown in the left-hand section of the picture. In the background the Japanese style wallpaper introduces a third cultural reference. Gauguin thus proposes in this painting a synthesis between three continents and three civilisations which he refuses to classify according to any hierarchy.

The work did not please its sitter, to whom the artist offered it: rejected by Angèle, it was acquired by Degas, who considered it to be a masterpiece.

50

Paul GAUGUIN

1848 – 1903

Autoportrait au Christ jaune

(1889-1890) ***Selfportrait with «Yellow Christ».*** This selfportrait, painted by Gauguin in 1889, shows an artist with an anguished face and reserved expression, against a background occupied by two of his recent works. On the left, the *Christ jaune (Yellow Christ)* is reversed because it is reflected in a mirror. It is often considered to be an image of the artist's destiny, sacrificed by and suffering for mankind. Here, however, Christ seems to be protecting Gauguin with his outstretched arm and sanctifying his creations.

The other work, represented on the right, is a ceramic pot, which is itself a selfportrait of the artist and also belongs to the Musée d'Orsay. Gauguin speaks of it as a «burned figure (...) poor devil turned in on himself to bear the suffering».

Placed between the two focus points represented by the *Christ jaune* and the pot, the artist's face impresses by its strength and determination. Maurice Denis, who purchased this picture, wrote concerning it: «It is firstly a balanced composition: Gauguin, who introduced so much disorder and incoherence into his life, did not tolerate it in his painting. He liked clarity, a sign of intelligence».

51

Paul GAUGUIN

1848 – 1903

Arearea

(1892) ***Arearea.*** Two young Tahitian girls are seated at the foot of a tree. One is playing a reed flute, the other listening with a dreamy expression. Around them, large patches of green and bright red, arabesque shaped plants, spots of colour, make up an exotic landscape steeped in a rather oppressive atmosphere of torpor. In the background, three women are dancing before a gigantic idol. The forms are simplified, the colours imaginary.

In the foreground a red dog is passing by. It amused or horrified the first spectators who saw the picture, but fascinated the Fauve painters and lead to the work being nicknamed *Chien rouge* (*Red dog*). However, Gauguin wrote *Arearea* on the canvas; this means «amusements» in Polynesian, a strange title in view of the melancholy which emanates from the picture.

Painted in 1892, during his first stay in Tahiti, this work was exhibited the following year in Paris. He was taken to task for the strangeness of his technique. He tried to explain it: «It is music, if you like! I obtain, by arrangements of lines and colours, with the pretext of some subject or other, symphonies, harmonies, representing nothing which is absolutely real in the common meaning of the word».

He set down in his paintings his dreams of virgin lands, of paradise lost, while at the same time noting in his diary: «But all that does not exist».

52

Georges SEURAT

1859 – 1891

Cirque

(1890-1891) ***Circus.*** *Cirque*
is Seurat's third picture on
contemporary popular
entertainments. Like Degas
and Toulouse-Lautrec, he was
interested in nocturnal scenes,
illuminated by electric light.

The surface of the canvas is vigorously
structured. In the foreground, the
curve of the ring is animated by a
series of spirals and arabesques:
those of the bareback rider, of the
acrobat leaping and bounding
behind her, of the ringmaster's
whip, or yet again of the clown's
costume. In the background, on
the contrary, the right-angle reigns
supreme with the horizontal lines
of the tiers of seats occupied by the
spectators, bolt upright like so
many Aunt Sallies. The contrast
between the exhilaration and
excitement of the show and the
rather starchy stillness of the
spectators is thus accentuated. The
absence of any impression of depth
is also striking: Seurat did not seek
to be realistic, all that interested
him was the combination of lines.
The colours are limited to two

dominant tones which reinforce each other: a warm orange-yellow and a cool violet-blue which is also found in the original painted frame. Black is completely absent whereas white makes its presence felt forcefully, all the more so since the painting is unfinished.

The small carefully applied brushstrokes follow the rhythm of the forms, making the surface of the canvas vibrate. This technique is typical of Divisionism, of which Seurat was the chief exponent.

53

Paul SIGNAC

1863 – 1935

La bouée rouge

(1895) ***The red buoy.*** While cruising in 1892 Paul Signac discovered the little port of St Tropez and was so enchanted that he bought a house there. The place inspired many of his works, including this *Bouée rouge*.

This picture can be compared with works of the Impressionist painters for several reasons: the choice of subject - houses along the harbour, a few sailing ships and, in the foreground, the buoy which gives its name to the painting - like the obvious desire to convey the play of light and shadow on water. However the technique used to apply the colour is quite different. Invented by Seurat, it played a role right from the beginning in the movement called Neo-Impressionism or Divisionism: instead of mixing colours on the palette before using them, the painter places dots of pure colour next to each other on the canvas: it is the spectator's eye which mixes them and recomposes the necessary synthesis.

However, between the 1880s and 1895,

Signac broadened his touch, which by now calls to mind a mosaic. As he said himself, «the touch is proportionate to the size of the picture».

Another difference compared with the work of the Impressionists: there is no longer any question of rendering the spontaneity of first impressions. All is carefully prepared; Signac did not paint directly out of doors, but in his studio from studies made on the spot.

54

Henri MATISSE

1869 – 1954

Luxe, calme et volupté

(1904) ***Luxury, peace and sensual indulgence.*** During the summer of 1904 Matisse stayed in St Tropez with the painter Signac, who was a little older than him and gladly welcomed younger artists. The atmosphere conveyed by this painting is that of a pastoral scene from classical antiquity, dominated by the warm range of colours used. Combining bathing women and a picnic, Matisse here sings the praises of an obviously Mediterranean nature but which is fantasised, freely retranscribed by means of a palette of imaginary tones. The title given to the work contributes to this sense of other-worldliness: it is taken from «L'invitation au voyage» («An invitation to travel»), a poem inspired by Holland in Baudelaire's *Fleurs du mal* : «Everything there is simply order and beauty, /Luxury, peace and sensual indulgence».

Shortly after painting this picture, which Signac kept in the dining-room of his house in St Tropez, Matisse turned to a broader and more synthetic style of painting.

55

Paul SÉRUSIER

1864 – 1927

Le talisman

(1888) ***The talisman.*** During the summer of 1888 Paul Sérusier joined some painter friends at Pont-Aven in Brittany. They were staying in the same inn as Gauguin. The latter agreed to give Sérusier a quick painting lesson in the small Bois d'Amour, situated near Pont-Aven.

Gauguin's advice, as reported by the painter Maurice Denis, was by and large as follows: «How do you see the trees? They are yellow, well, put yellow there; the shadow is bluish, paint it with pure ultramarine».

When Sérusier returned to Paris with his small panel, he showed it to his friends. It was a real revelation for this group of young artists who were seeking a different path from that of the Impressionists. They wished to return to the sacred nature of painting and called themselves the «Nabis», which means «prophets» in Hebrew. Maurice Denis, the group's theorist, stated: «Remember that a picture, before being a war horse, a naked woman, or any kind of anecdote, is essentially a flat surface covered with colours assembled in a certain order». And that is indeed what this small panel is, depicting trees, a path, a house, water, reflections in the water, all treated in flat blocks of colour, with no relief.

Denis and Bonnard, joined by Vuillard and Vallotton, hung the painting on the wall of the room where they met and which they called «the Temple». It was considered an icon and was soon given the title *Talisman*, which well reflects the important role it played in the history of art.

56

Salle des fêtes

Reception room. Orsay railway
station, which was to be
transformed in 1978 into a museum
for the art of the period between
1848 and 1914, was inaugurated in
1900 at the time of the Universal
Exhibition. Its often inventive
metallic structures, hidden under a
cladding of stone and stucco, make
it a good example of late 19th
century academic architecture.
Built by the architect Victor Laloux,
the station was surrounded by a
luxurious hotel. On the first floor
of the building were large
reception rooms, in particular all
along the façade overlooking Rue
de Bellechasse, where today the
museum restaurant is situated.

The hotel's «salle des fêtes» (literally,
«room for festivities») overlooked
the Seine. Crystal chandeliers and
festooned lights, reflected by huge
mirrors, illuminate the room
brilliantly. An important painted
ceiling and four overdoors,
commissioned for the hotel, still

bear witness to its luxury. It was intended not only for travellers passing through the city, but also for special occasions celebrated by Parisians.

This room now serves as one of the museum galleries, housing examples of 19th century academic sculpture. It is also sometimes used for concerts.

57

Jean-Paul AUBÉ

1837 – 1916

Monument à Léon Gambetta

(1884) *Memorial for Léon Gambetta.* The Third Republic was proclaimed by Gambetta in 1870: the Prussian army had just beaten that of Napoleon III. During the 1880s it tried to establish its legitimacy by launching a vast programme of monuments in honour of great men and republican ideals.

After Gambetta's death a fund was started to erect a memorial to him. It was intended to recall the reasons for Gambetta's place in history: the founding of the third French Republic and his role in the defence of the nation. Eighty projects were proposed. The one designed by the architect Boileau and the sculptor Aubé won the competition.

The memorial experienced a turbulent history. First installed in a courtyard at the Louvre it was damaged and displaced several times. What is left of it has been installed since 1982 near Place Gambetta in Paris.

It consists of a base bearing a pylon; a statue of Gambetta stands out against its principal face. Inspired by Rude's group on the Arc de Triomphe at the Place de l'Étoile, the great man seems to be urging the Nation on to a supreme effort in defence of the invaded motherland. His left arm is around a wounded soldier who symbolises the exhausted army. At his feet, a youth stoops to pick up a weapon. A workman with a wiry torso holds the butt of a gun in both hands. Under the group two cherubs frame the plaque bearing the dedication: «A Gambetta, la Patrie et la République» («To Gambetta, the Motherland and the Republic»).

58

Fernand-Anne PIESTRE

called CORMON

1845 – 1924

Caïn

(1880) «When, with his children clad in animals' pelts, Dishevelled, livid in the midst of storms, Cain fled from the face of Jehovah (...)»

Cain. These three lines by Victor Hugo accompanied the title of the picture in the booklet for the 1880 Salon. This monumental painting shows Cain, with a melancholy expression, his sacrilegious axe tied at his hip, leading his clan towards an unknown destiny, fleeing God's wrath after the murder of his brother. The long shadows, the barren ground and the heavy sky compose a desolate background against which the muscular bodies stand out clearly.

Beyond its biblical and moral dimension, this work plunges the spectator into the very heart of the disturbing universe of primitive life. Throughout his life Cormon was interested in the mysteries of human evolution. He invented a genre: the representation of prehistory in painting. Bringing together biblical texts and anthropological research, he described in detail things which, for lack of documentation, could not be other than reinvented. He used the techniques specific to historical painting, traditionally considered as a noble genre.

These references to the Bible or to Victor Hugo, who was hugely popular at the time, together with this encounter between the imaginary and the scientific concerns of the period, ensured an immense success for this work.

59

Édouard DETAILLE

1848 – 1912

Le rêve

(1888) ***The dream.*** This monumental work met with stunning success and was widely circulated at the time through numerous reproductions. It expressed to perfection the patriotic consciousness of the French and their desire for revenge after the defeat of 1870.

The bivouacking French army is shown full of the promise of dawn and of victory. It is young, well-trained, well-equipped, as proved by the piles of arms, and well-commanded – the officers are close to their men. They can be seen in the left foreground, clearly distinguishable because of their gloves, embroidered headgear and swords planted in the ground.

Represented in the form of a heavenly vision, *Le rêve* is a parade through the hosts of legendary armies which had made France illustrious over the previous hundred years.

The armies from the Revolution to
the Second Empire, recognisable
by their flags and uniforms, are
successively passed in review.
This picture sought to heal the patriotic
wound of 1870 by exalting the
unity of the nation and its trust in
its army.

60

Jules DALOU

1838 – 1902

Grand paysan
(1889-1899) *Large peasant.*

This *Grand paysan*, with its simple style devoid of any grandiloquence, is an example of research into realism in sculpture. The man is looking at the ground, where his legs seem almost to be planted. His sleeves are rolled up, he is about to begin his task, «forehead down, like that of a draught ox».

This sculpture was intended for a *Monument au travail* (*Monument to work*) begun in 1889, by which the artist wished to exalt the condition of the working man. Dalou had prepared many studies, but the monument was never executed. Like his *Forgeron* (*Blacksmith*), this *Grand paysan* bears witness to the appearance in sculpture of a concept which already had antecedents in literature and painting: the realistic portrayal of humble people depicted in their daily toil, but elevated to the rank of heroes.

In so doing, it broke completely with the classical conventions which governed sculpture, like painting, and consisted of placing peasants in a mythological or allegorical context.

61

Sir Edward BURNE-JONES

1833 – 1898

La roue de la fortune

(1875-1885) ***The wheel of Fortune.*** This picture represents the allegorical figure of Fortune turning a wheel to which are attached three figures: a slave at the top, a king in the middle and a poet at the bottom – images of the fate of mankind, passing from glory to oblivion, from riches to poverty. «My *Wheel of Fortune* is a true picture; it seeks us each out in turn, then crushes us», Burne-Jones wrote.

This artist's name is associated with the Pre-Raphaelites, one of the first Symbolist movements, which appeared in Great Britain in 1848 under the influence of Dante Gabriel Rossetti. The members of the «Pre-Raphaelite Brotherhood» proclaimed their rejection of reality and their desire to return to Gothic art, to Italian 15th century painting and to all that preceded Raphael. However, Michelangelo remained an essential reference for Burne-Jones.

In this painting, the figure of Fortune is inspired by the Sibyl on the ceiling of the Sixtine Chapel. The male nudes adopt the poses of the dying slaves and captives sculpted by Michelangelo. The work is moreover reminiscent of a bas-relief, since the colours are restricted to tones of brown for the wheel and the three men and of grey for the monumental figure of Fortune, whose draperies call to mind armour. This painting, completed in 1883, was exhibited in London where it met with great success. A little later it was admired in France by Puvis de Chavannes and his contemporaries.

62

Gustav KLIMT

1862 – 1918

Rosiers sous les arbres

(c. 1905) ***Rose bushes under trees.***

In this work the Austrian artist Gustav Klimt transforms a landscape into a mosaic composed of a swarming homogeneous mass of plants occupying almost the whole of the surface of the canvas. The only elements introducing any variation are the parallel motifs formed by the rose bushes and the tree trunks. The discreet allusion, on the right, to a very high skyline establishes a certain impression of depth, contrasting with the foliage which is both very flat and very close to the spectator.

The artist's taste for decoration is obvious: the square format of the picture favours its treatment in the style of a piece of fabric, by small touches of colour. At the same time, the work radiates vitality, and the quest for a true to life atmosphere links it with the preoccupations which had fascinated the Impressionists.

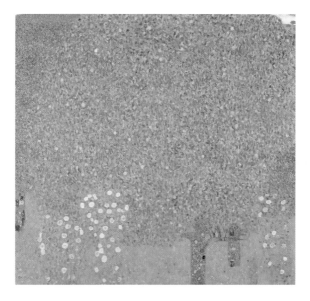

63

René LALIQUE

1860 – 1945

Flacon à odeur

(c. 1900-1902) *Scent bottle.*

René Lalique, first known as a
jeweller, introduced glass elements
into his jewellery during the last
years of the 19th century before
becoming a famous master
glassmaker after 1900, doubtless
stimulated by Gallé's success.
This small scent bottle was intended to
be carried around by its owner.
The cast and chased gold stopper
called on techniques used by
goldsmiths. The bottle itself is
made of glass moulded by the cire
perdue, or lost-wax, method, using
a technique developed by Lalique
and based on bronze sculpture: the
piece is modelled in wax, then
covered with heat-resistant clay
before being placed in a furnace.
The wax melts and runs away; it is
then replaced by molten glass.
This technique, simple in theory, is
very complicated in practice, and
was kept secret. The result is a
precious substance, reminiscent of
rock crystal, perfectly suited to
small objects of this type. Its

decoration is inspired from marine flora and fauna: fish are encrusted in the glass body, while seaweed enhances the gold stopper.

There are only a very few examples of bottles made by this technique for a well-to-do clientele.

64

Odilon REDON

1840 – 1916

Ensemble de panneaux décoratifs

(1901) ***Set of decorative panels.***

These twelve panels painted by Odilon Redon in 1901 were part of a set commissioned from him to decorate the dining-room of a private château. Their forceful decorative style recalls the great compositions of Puvis de Chavannes or those of Édouard Vuillard for the interiors of Parisian art lovers.

However, in this case there is no real subject. The colour explodes, as it were, dominated by the yellow chosen by the client. Forms – real or invented – disintegrate there, close to Redon's usual register, but devoid of the feeling of anxiety previously noted.

«I am covering the walls of a dining-room with flowers,» he wrote, «dream flowers, large panels treated with a bit of everything, tempera, oils, pastels, with which I have good results for the time being.»

This set of panels was the first of a series which occupied the artist until the end of his life.

65

François-Rupert Carabin

1862 – 1932

Bibliothèque

(1890) **Bookcase.** In response to a collector's commission, Carabin worked for nearly a year on the design and execution of this bookcase, which he was later to consider as one of his most successful creations in the domain of furniture. The visual conception of the piece, decorated with sculptures carved in the round, is well suited to its rich symbolism: near the ground are found personifications of passions which are the enemies of Intelligence – Ignorance, Vanity, Greed, Intemperance, Anger, Stupidity and Hypocrisy – vanquished and reduced to slavery by books, whereas, right at the top, two quiet figures representing Reading sit on either side of Truth.

Virulently opposed to the industrial production of furniture which had become widespread at the end of the 19th century, Carabin, a former craftsman, preached strongly in favour of a return to traditional work. The young Art Nouveau creators shared his taste for natural wood. However his use of embellishments and sculpture pushed, as is the case here, to the limits of the unusual, distinguish him from artists who were above all concerned with the functional aspects of furniture.

66

Émile GALLÉ

1846 – 1904

La main aux algues et aux coquillages

(1904) **Hand with seaweed and shells.** In 1904 Gallé finished *La main aux algues et aux coquillages*. While the three hundred employees in his Nancy workshop made mass-produced pieces, Gallé continued to create decorative objects executed in a very limited number of copies, for which he called on a small team of extremely competent and faithful glass-blowers and engravers.

Gallé doubtless found sources of inspiration in recent discoveries concerning the underwater world which had revealed what he called «the enamels and cameos of the sea». The principal element of this work is engraved crystal, shot through with inclusions. It is enhanced with polychrome applications: the shells which decorate the hand like rings and the seaweed wrapped around it. The varying thickness of the glass paste leads to a play between opaque and translucid sections which evokes ocean depths. Did Gallé have in mind ex-votos from

classical antiquity? Did he intend
to evoke the Asian religions, of
which Europe was rediscovering
the major texts? Or is the
incantatory and protective gesture
of this hand linked to the artist's
personal situation: he was ill and
this was doubtless his last creation
in glass?

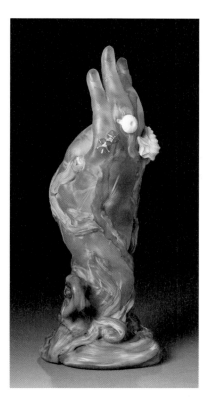

67

Hector Guimard

1867 – 1942

Banquette de fumoir

(1897) ***Bench for a smoking-room.***
Hector Guimard, famous for the
entrances he designed for the Paris
Métro, is also known for his apartment buildings and private houses.
He was an architect, but also carefully considered the interior design
and furnishings. This bench har-
monises with the architecture and
almost blends in with it: the ornamental wooden structure which
extends it, inspired by some creep-
er, is like panelling placed behind
it; a small glass-doored cupboard
nestles high up in one of its
branches, prolonged by three stems
bearing a roof.

Were possible users put off by the
unusual motifs or the general
dissymmetry? The difficulty of
placing such a piece of furniture
near others, designed in
accordance with different
principles, may explain the
unpopularity of Art Nouveau
furniture after World War I.

68

Pierre BONNARD

1867 – 1947

Femmes au jardin

(1891) ***Women in a garden.*** «The folding screen has been broken up ... I have made four separate panels from it. They look much better

against a wall. It was too much of a picture for a screen», Bonnard wrote to his mother in March 1891 about *Femmes au jardin*. A few weeks later, he presented the decorative panels at the Salon des Indépendants. The artist, then aged twenty-four, played an active role in defining the Nabis' aesthetic principles, with their dual concern: creating decorative art and not restricting themselves to easel paintings. *Femmes au jardin* represent the first truly Nabi decorative ensemble.

The influence of Japan is obvious. In 1890 Bonnard saw an exhibition of Japanese art at the Paris fine arts school. He has adopted the tall format of kakemonos (hanging vertical scrolls) used by Japanese artists. Like them, he has flattened forms and reduced figures to mere silhouettes applied against a background. He has given no impression of depth, but contrasted light and dark tones and played on arabesques and straight lines. *Femmes au jardin* thus justifies Bonnard's nickname of «Nabi très japonard» (very «Japanesey» Nabi).

69

Henry Van de Velde

1863 – 1957

Écritoire

(1898-1899) ***Writing-desk.*** This *Writing-desk* by Henry Van de Velde gives an impression of great simplicity. The material used for this complex piece of furniture - natural wood - is not disguised by being covered with marquetry or given any colour very different from that of oak.

Moreover, its very restrained decoration is totally part of it, and seems designed to endorse its shape. For example, the gilt bronze handles of the drawers symmetrically direct the eye back to the centre of the desk, to its heart, to its very function. Whereas at the end of the 19th century many pieces of furniture still bore heavy, if masterly, fittings with no relationship to their form, for Van de Velde, as for many of the best Art Nouveau creators, form and ornaments were inseparable. This trend towards greater simplicity was soon to mark developments in the domains of both furniture and architecture.

70

Alexandre CHARPENTIER

1856 – 1909

Salle à manger

(1900-1901) ***Dining-room.*** This *Dining-room*, commissioned from Charpentier by a banker for his country residence, provides an example of close collaboration between representatives of different branches of the decorative arts in order to create a coherent whole.

The wood panelling, carved with climbing plants, incorporates two sideboards, two silver cabinets situated in the corners and a large stoneware basin. The latter was the work of the ceramist Bigot, who also made the frieze of tiles covering the tops of the walls. In addition to the table the room also held a set of furniture which has now disappeared but which comprised twenty-four chairs, a chandelier and wall-lights.

Designing an interior as a global and coherent project was one of the characteristics of Art Nouveau, a reaction against the juxtaposition of very diverse elements and styles, typical of what has been called Eclecticism.

The sheer magnitude of such projects helps to explain why Art Nouveau was so often reserved for a private clientele composed of rich patrons.

71

Auguste RODIN

1840 – 1917

La Pensée

(1886-1889) ***Thought.*** *La Pensée*
was modelled by Rodin in 1886
then, as was the practice of the
time, carved in marble by an assist-
ant. The artist had already tackled
this subject when he created his
very famous *Penseur* (*The Thinker*),
where the essential lay in the attitude: the whole Herculean body
expressed thought with a dramatically powerful intensity.

There is nothing similar in this small
strong but delicate marble
sculpture. Camille Claudel, the
artist's pupil and mistress, served
as the model. The head is young,
with delicate features. She is
leaning forward, in shadow; it is
impossible to meet her eyes. There
is nothing tragic here, she is as if
lost in a daydream, to the point of
herself becoming that dreamy
thought. That is why this statue
has sometimes been called a
symbolistic work: it is like the
symbol of thought emerging from
unformed material, illustrated by
the strong contrast between the
smooth face and the gangue from
which it is emerging.

72

Camille CLAUDEL

1864 – 1943

L'âge mûr

(1899-1903) ***Middle Age.*** For the
writer Paul Claudel, this work by
his sister Camille summed up the
drama of her life: «This young
naked girl is my sister. My sister
Camille, imploring, humiliated, on
her knees. And do you know, what
is being torn away from her at this
very moment under our eyes is her
soul». In fact, the sculpture
probably represents her break with
Rodin. Camille is leaning forward
to try and retain her lover, but
Rodin is carried off by his
longstanding companion, Rose
Beuret, whom he had never wished
to leave.

The composition of the group is
asymmetric, and this imbalance
underlines the gap between the
young girl's hands and her lover's.
He has already turned away from
her; his movement, his body,
showing his age, his face with its
blurred features, all express
helpless resignation. As for Rose,
she is depicted as a gaunt old
woman. The heavy drapery
billowing out from her shoulders
makes her resemble the angel of

death. In fact, the group is sometimes given the title *Les âges de la Vie* (*The ages of life*) for, beyond Camille's personal drama, it can also be considered as representing Old Age carrying a middle-aged man towards his destiny despite the entreaties of Youth.

The sculpture was executed in 1899, shortly after the break between Rodin and his pupil. The following years were to be like a slow descent into hell for Camille, leading to madness and internment from 1913 until her death in 1943.

73

Auguste RODIN

1840 – 1917

Porte de l'Enfer

(1880-1917) *Gate of Hell.* In 1880 the State commissioned from Rodin a monumental door for a museum of decorative arts which was to be erected on the present site of the Musée d'Orsay. The museum was never to be built, but Rodin worked until 1917 on the *Porte de l'Enfer* . All available space is occupied by a tormented background of figures suddenly appearing from nowhere or returning there, as if snatched up by some perpetual whirlwind. Inspired by Dante's *Divine Comedy* some two hundred damned souls are entangled with one another in this horrific universe. Most of them have also led a separate existence, either before or after being used in this *Gate.* At the top, the *Trois ombres* (*Three Shades*) take up the form of Adam's silhouette, seen from three different angles, their left arms pointing towards the principal figure: *Le penseur* (*The thinker*). He is contemplating the giddy whirling and fall of this blighted mankind. Behind him are the crowd of damned souls of the first circle of hell. On the left-hand section of the door, at the bottom, the tragic lovers, Paolo and Francesca, can be seen. Above them, Ugolino in the midst of his children represents man degraded by suffering. The *Porte de l'Enfer* was constantly reworked by Rodin who, for thirty-seven years, added, displaced or broke the fragments which he gradually assembled. He sought the expressiveness of the bodies, obtaining spectacular effects of light and shadow by resorting in turn to flowing curves or to brutality in the modelling. This ambitious work remained unfinished. But, in Rodin's words, «Are cathedrals ever finished?».

74

Auguste RODIN

1840 – 1917

Ugolin

(1882-1906) ***Ugolino.*** Dante, in his *Divine Comedy,* tells of the punishment inflicted on Count Ugolino in Pisa during the 13th century. Having betrayed the Ghibellines, he was imprisoned with his children and condemned to death by starvation. Since his children died before him, he ate their corpses, which earned him eternal damnation.

In 1862 Carpeaux represented Ugolino seated, surrounded by his children, biting his fingers in despair.

Rodin addressed a later episode of the story: Ugolino's children are already lying lifeless around him. «Myself, already blind, from one to the other felt my way: three days I called them after they were dead. (...) Then, hunger was stronger than sorrow.»

Rodin's interpretation of the drama shows the blind father's haggard face, emphasising his helplessness and despair as he loses all human dignity before sinking into bestiality.

75

Auguste RODIN

1840 – 1917

Balzac

(1897) **Balzac.** The «Société des gens de lettres» (Society of men of letters) wished to erect a monument in memory of Balzac. One was commissioned from Chapu, but he died shortly afterwards. Zola then managed to have the commission given to Rodin.

For six years the artist made countless studies. In particular he executed an astonishing series of nudes whose frequently exaggerated forms sought to render the force of Balzac's genius. The sculptor Pompon, who worked in his studio, recounted: «He wanted to make a sort of term, or pillar, with a head on it. He first made a magnificent study of a nude. When he had finished it, Rodin dipped his dressing gown in a large basin of plaster and clothed his study in it. I find it magnificent».

According to Élie Faure (a French essayist, historian of art and critic), the statue is «like those menhirs which elementary forces seem to erect along our paths». Actually, with the lines of the gown leading towards the huge head the work is an almost abstract symbol of the novelist's force. Totally at variance with traditional public monuments, it created such a scandal that Rodin lost the commission. It was only in 1939 that a bronze cast of the statue was erected in Paris, on Boulevard Raspail.

76

Émile-Antoine BOURDELLE

1861 – 1929

Héraklès tue les oiseaux du lac Stymphale

(1909) ***Herakles killing the birds of the Lake Stymphalis.*** Émile Bourdelle, one of Rodin's former pupils, returned to the representation of mythological figures. This gilt bronze statue is his most famous work. It represents one of the twelve labours of Hercules (Herakles in Greek): Eurystheus asked Herakles to destroy the birds who were so numerous that they threatened the surrounding countryside. The hero brought them down with his arrows.

When it was presented at the 1910 Salon, the work created a sensation. Critics noted the bold style and tension of the figure. «The incredibly daring movement of this athlete in equilibrium in thin air, braced against the top of a rock, this member of the human race who seems to be leaping in his very immobility, the summary but accurate and vibrant modelling,

this is one of the most prodigious undertakings of living art.»
There was also a lot said about the head, «stern and terrifying, which expresses fierce determination and wily calculation, the head of a cruel and covetous conquistador». Finally, the simplicity of the work was praised: «Before this admirable *Hercules* (...) there is no need to rack one's brains to understand».

77

Aristide MAILLOL

1861 – 1944

Méditerranée

(1905) ***The Mediterranean.*** «It is beautiful, it signifies nothing; it is a silent work. I believe one must go far back in time to find such a complete lack of any concern other than the simple manifestation of beauty.» That is how André Gide, in his review of the 1905 Salon d'Automne, where Maillol presented the plaster for *Méditerranée*, rendered homage to this as yet unknown sculptor, for whom it was the first success. After having practised painting and weaving, Maillol turned to sculpture at the age of forty, as he was threatened with blindness.

This woman, seated in a meditative attitude, was his first large sculpture. Both serene and serious, shut in on herself, there is an equilibrium between the masses which gives perfect stability to the whole. The motionless body is inscribed in a cube, the forms are full and smooth, the rhythms supple, and the volumes have harmonious curves. In complete contrast to Rodin's tormented and tumultuous style of art, Maillol simplifies modelling to the extreme in the pursuit of calm and plenitude.

It was in 1923 that the State commissioned the marble version exhibited in the Musée d'Orsay.

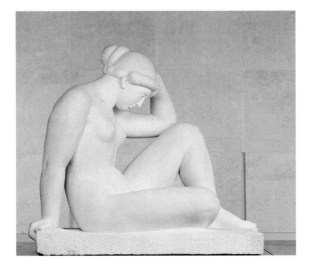

78

François POMPON

1855 – 1933

Ours blanc

(1922-1925) ***Polar bear.*** *Ours blanc* is probably François Pompon's best-known work. It marked the start of his success at the 1923 Salon d'Automne, when he was already sixty-seven. Orders poured in and until 1933 *Polar bears* were made in all sizes and all types of material: biscuit-ware, porcelain, bronze, marble or stone, like this one.

François Pompon belonged to the «Société des sculpteurs animaliers» (Society of sculptors of animals). It is said that at the Jardin des Plantes (Paris botanical gardens) he followed the animals around and modelled their movements straight away in clay, on a small workbench which he carried slung around his neck. He then worked on these sketches in his studio, eliminating all details, hair, fur or feathers, scraping the surface in order to retain only smooth and simple shapes, over which light would glide. This heavy and solid *Ours blanc* seems to have been cut out in a single piece from a block of ice. It is completely contained in an outline which the artist is said to have drawn with one continuous stroke. Pompon said: «It is funny, an animal does not have an end. That means (...) that its outline has to form a loop, it must be enclosed in its own shape».

79

Maurice DENIS

1870 – 1943

Les Muses

(1893) ***The Muses.*** In spite of the title of the picture, there is nothing mythological about these young women, gathered under some chestnut trees. Their hairstyles and clothing belong resolutely to the contemporary world, the setting is a public garden with its iron seats. Moreover, it is impossible to identify all the Muses. At the very most one can recognise, in the group in the foreground, Melpomene, the Muse of Tragedy, dressed in black, and Calliope, the Muse of Epic Poetry, busy sharpening her pencil.

The strong likeness between the figures is striking: Maurice Denis, in painting them, was inspired by his young wife Martha, «his» Muse. Their treatment emphasises this similarity even more: each one is surrounded by a smooth simplified contour.

The trees, like the leaves scattered on the ground, are also stylised. The deep matt colours, like the soft and mysterious atmosphere, accentuate the decorative nature of the work.

80

Pierre BONNARD

1867 – 1947

La partie de croquet ou Crépuscule

(1892) ***The game of croquet*** or ***Twilight.*** In the green suffocating heat of this family garden, the eye first perceives a few forms: the man and woman on the left with the dog, the young girls dancing a round further to the right, and the colours of the setting sun through the trees. In fact, on the left there are four people, for a man and a woman in checked clothes emerge from the shadow like vignettes affixed to the background of greenery.

There are therefore two scenes, side by side but completely foreign to each other. On the left, the static croquet players are treated like a decorative frieze of silhouettes with no substance. On the right, the mobile and sinuous figures of the young girls are treated in solid blocks of colour.

The viewpoint changes for each group, there are multiple perspectives: we are above the bushes in the foreground, but below the space where the young girls are twirling round. This disposition with several viewpoints is inspired by Japanese art, which the Nabis knew well; Japanese influence is also obvious in the treatment of the feminine silhouettes and the way in which the bushes are cut off by the lower edge of the canvas. Maurice Denis, on this question, wrote: «Mr Bonnard «Japanises» in a very personal way». This picture, with its overriding attention to the decorative aspect, is a perfect illustration of the Nabis' aesthetic principles.

81

Édouard VUILLARD

1868 – 1940

Jardins publics

(1894)   ***Public gardens.*** These five
panels belong to a set of nine
which are now dispersed. They
were commissioned from Vuillard
in 1894 by Alexandre Natanson, the
editor of *La Revue blanche.* This
publication, founded at the end of
the 19th century, encouraged
various avant-garde artistic and
literary movements, in particular
that of the Nabis, to which Vuillard
belonged.

The painter did not refer here to any specific public garden, but rather made a synthesis of his impressions of different Paris parks: the Bois de Boulogne, the Parc de Saint-Cloud and the Tuileries garden. Heir to Puvis de Chavannes by the magnitude of the mural composition, and to Monet by the impression of being in the open air, Vuillard also drew inspiration from Japanese prints for the very elongated format of his panels. Each one can be considered as an independent composition, but also as part of a whole. In order to adapt his work to the light of the room in which the panels were to be placed Vuillard used distemper, which gives a matt aspect similar to that of frescos.

82

Félix VALLOTTON

1865 – 1925

Le ballon

(1899) **The ball.** On a sunny esplanade a child is running after a red ball; its silhouette, composed of a few blocks of colour, stands out against the sand. Behind, in the dense shadow of a park, two tiny female figures appear in a thin ray of light.

The scene is enigmatic: the women seem far away, suggesting a great depth in the space. However, all perspective seems lacking. To achieve this impression, Vallotton had recourse to two stratagems: on the one hand, he adopted a raised viewpoint for the foreground, beyond which the ground rises to a fairly high horizon, and on the other hand he has banished the sky from his composition, obliging himself to make the scene coincide with the plane of the canvas: a picture is a flat surface. Two year earlier, Vallotton had been encouraged by the Nabis in his desire to work in a decorative style. In this painting the forms are simplified to the extreme and treated in coloured masses. But beyond any decorative considerations, one already has the feeling of the evocation of atmosphere which was to lead the artist in later works towards the representation of magical landscapes animated by obscure forces.

order of the visit

ground floor
upper level
middle level

access

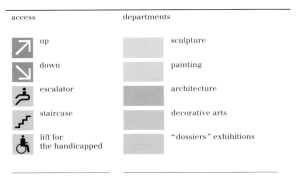

↗ up

↘ down

escalator

staircase

lift for
the handicapped

departments

sculpture

painting

architecture

decorative arts

"dossiers" exhibitions

services

 toilets

 cloakroom
for individuals

 cloakroom
for groups

telephone

post

 audioguide

restaurant service

reception desk

room numbers

59 the numbers marked on
this map are also indicated
on the room signs of the
museum

ground floor

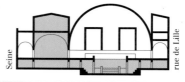

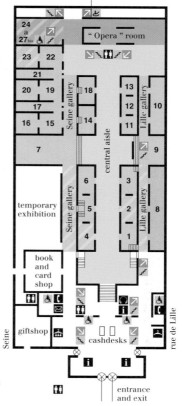

upper level

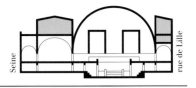

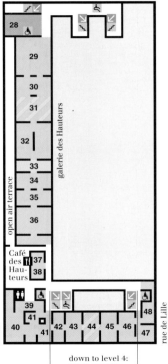

down to level 4:
press corridor
49 photographs
50 Kaganovitch
collection

middle level

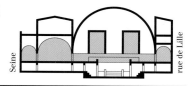

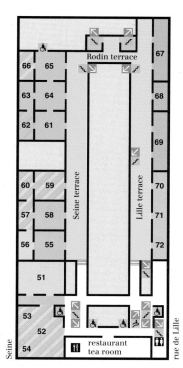

Authors: Claire Barbillon, Joëlle Bolloch, Stéphane Guégan, Nicole Hodcent, Françoise Le Coz, Laurence Madeline, Jérôme Picon, Anne Pingeot, Nicole Savy, Pierre Sesmat, Frédéric Sorbier, Araxie Toutghalian

Photographic credits:
Réunion des musées nationaux
(D. Arnaudet,
M. Bellot, G. Blot,
H. Lewandowski,
R. G. Ojéda)

Published by the Département des éditions directed by
Anne de Margerie

Editorial coordination: Claire Barbillon and Jérôme Picon (Musée d'Orsay), Céline Julhiet-Charvet (Réunion des musées nationaux)

Design: Cécile Neuville

Plans designed by: C. Le Trung, C. Lebrun (Musée d'Orsay)

Production: Jacques Venelli

This book was printed and bound in March 2001 by imprimerie Kapp Lahure Jombart, Évreux. Photoengraving for illustrations by Dry, Montreuil-sous-Bois. Acknowlegements to : Sycomore

1ᵉʳ dépôt légal : mai 1998

Dépôt légal : mars 2001

cover Illustrations :
Edgar Degas, *Dans un café* (n° 31) ; Édouard Manet, *Olympia* (n° 19) ; Vincent Van Gogh, *Portrait de l'artiste* (n° 46) ; Paul Gauguin, *Arearea* (n° 51).